# A Daily Dose of Inspiration

**Peaches Joy Williams**

Peaches Joy Williams

Author contact: peachesjoy.ptp@hotmail.com

Cover design by Joel Rowe

**Copyright Year:** April 2017

**Copyright Notice:** by Peaches Joy Williams. All rights reserved. No part of this book may be reproduced in any form or by any means whatsoever.

Results in this copyright notice:
© *2017 Peaches Joy Williams. All rights reserved*

**ISBN: 978-1-909389-15-1**

## Dedications

To my children, Christina, Shannon and Joel who have been with me on this journey, I Love You. To my friends, Paula Burton and Dambile Nkunika - Peters, who encouraged and supported me in every way from the very beginning. To my family, especially my sisters, Sharon Williams and Janice Williams, you both have been my Cheerleaders. To friends who offered a helping hand and a listening ear. I Thank You all for your Love.

# What Inspired me to write...

## A Daily Dose of Inspiration

In February 2010 I made a life changing decision to walk away from my marriage after 17 years. That was an extremely difficult decision to make for me since I had walked away twice before. This time, however, I was sure that this was going to be the third and last time as I knew beyond any doubt that I needed to have my PEACE above all else. It was that choice which set the stage for all the drama, persecution and contentions I had to deal with over the next five years. It meant that I lost custody of my children, lost my home, faced charges, was jailed on three occasions, with possible long-term incarceration. But, I stood trial for five days in Snaresbrook Crown Court where I represented myself...and won.

During two and a half years, I appeared at three different courts over 80 times and answered charges of harassment and four injunction breaches. I cried so many nights until my head constantly hurt and my eyes, swollen; many nights hungry in a cold house in the middle of winter, I went to bed hungry. It was during those tumultuous times and victorious moments that I wrote most of these quotes.

Yes, the rough road and valley experiences have made me stronger, and for me, I am better and definitely WISER.

# A Daily Dose of Inspiration

*"The world is filled with stories, each and every single day. You too have a story...one the world is waiting to hear, WRITE IT!"*

**Kwame MA McPherson**

**Award-winning Writer, Content Organiser and Book Architect**
www.kwamemcpherson.com

# A Daily Dose of Inspiration

## Quotes and Thoughts to Inspire

*A Daily Dose of Inspiration: Quotes and Thoughts to Inspire* was inspired by the challenges and persecution I faced after a marriage break up. It was conceived from the encouragement of friends and family who thanked me for my quotes and thoughts which I posted daily on social media and also sent via messages to them during times of hardships and trials. It aims to Inspire and Encourage anyone who lacks self-belief and confidence or thinks of Giving Up.

*A Daily Dose of Inspiration: Quotes and Thoughts to Inspire* speaks to you from the heart and from very real experiences.

Peaches Joy Williams

"As you walk into your Destiny and Transform into the Amazing person you are, some things will fall away from your life, some of these will be bad habits, your friends, your doubts, your fears or even your family. Do not try to pick them up...they were not meant to be a part of your Destiny."

PJW

# Contents

| | |
|---|---|
| Acknowledgements | 10 |
| Introduction | 11 |
| About Love... | 13 |
| About Life... | 21 |
| About Relationships... | 51 |
| About Self-Belief... | 59 |
| About Being Yourself... | 67 |
| About Dreams and Goals... | 76 |
| About Life Lessons... | 84 |
| About Peace of Mind... | 98 |
| My Butterfly | 102 |
| About The Author: Peaches Joy Williams | 103 |

## Acknowledgements

During the last seven years I have had many challenges but the opportunity to meet many wonderful people who have helped and supported me on my journey, has been fantastic and a blessing. A few have gone the extra mile and they are the ones I would like to thank; for the role they have played and continue to play in my life.
I would like to thank my dear friend, Valda Bernard-Jones who kept believing in me; to Yetunde Olomolaiye who constantly encouraged me; to Megan Peterson who believed in my potential to be great and to do great things; to my friend Esther Brown who, since our University days, always encouraged, nudged and reminded me of my magnificent talents; to my biggest, loudest, longest cheerleader, Doreen Thelwell – love you loads.
I would like to also thank Kwame MA McPherson, my content organiser and book architect, who assisted me in bringing this book to reality, fine-tuning the small details and rough edges while supporting me in launching myself as an authentic author.
And to all those who I have not mentioned, the list is inexhaustive to write and would be another book in itself.
To you all, I give Thanks.

## Introduction

For all my life I have always been a smart talker or as Jamaicans often say *"fullah mout' or fullah chat"*. I however did not start to truly blossom or understand life's mysteries until I started experiencing gut wrenching pain, intense heartache, unwavering troubles, tumultuous trials, painful persecution, rejection and groundless betrayal. They say experience teaches wisdom and that is truly a fact, but it is evidenced by the birth of a new attitude towards life and a sense of peace in times of troubles, coupled with a greater knowledge and understanding of people and their behaviours.

As we walk along life's journey we learn to let go of things that hold us down or back, we gain wisdom from those painful experiences and certainly lose or gain friends who impact upon our lives. And whether the experience is bad or good, we emerge from it a different person, with a greater knowledge and a deeper insight from the lessons learnt; just so we never repeat them yet never to forget them either.

This book of quotes and thoughts has come to you simply because these are the lessons I have learnt, are relevant as well as thought provoking. They explain my journey and experiences in so many different areas – in my friendships, my intimate relationships, my struggles, my career and through the Justice System (a total of 82 times in three years).

I hope while you read these thoughts they resonate with you, so you too can experience a deeper sense of who you are, who you ought to be and enhance your attitude towards life and people. I hope you are awakened by each word from my thoughts.

Thank you for using your precious time to read *'A Daily Dose of Inspiration: Quotes and Thoughts to Inspire'*.

I sincerely HOPE you are truly INSPIRED.

Peaches Joy

## About Love...

"There is nothing more precious than Love, nothing more Valuable. Soon enough humankind will realise, Love is the only solution to every problem there is on earth"

PJW

"If they truly love you they will accept you with all your flaws. If they do not, they will keep pointing them out until you feel inadequate. Remember, those who love you will make you love yourself."

*Think on This:*

*Someone who really cares about you will not spend time with you pointing out what is wrong with you. Instead, what they will do is compliment you on the attributes which make you special, will keep reminding you of them and will work with you on the flaws.*

"Walk away from those who expect you to be perfect and hold you to their standard of perfection. If they love you they will love your imperfections."

*Think on This:*

*No one is perfect, if they expect you to be then they are expecting too much.*

"Many people will not love you, in fact many will not even like you. Just be reminded that the Art of Loving begins with loving yourself."

*Think on This:*
*If you truly love yourself then you will not be bothered by anyone else not loving you.*

"Yes, it hurts,

Yes, it is painful,

Yes, sometimes no one but you understand,

Yes, you still love even though you do not want to,

Sometimes, the release you need is just a few steps away,

Always be strengthened by it,

Sometimes, you just have to walk away and let it GO."

"Some will hate you because you have wronged them, some will hate you because others love you. Always remember an ounce of Love is STRONGER than a pound of hate."

*Think on This:*

*Those who hate you because others love you, have a problem with loving themselves. Do not ever make it about you.*

"Cherish the ones who smile at your good fortune and console you when you are saddened. Go where the Love is. They are the real deal."

*Think on This:*

*There are people in your life who will never rejoice with you because they never want to see you happy. Keep in mind the saying, "misery loves company".*

"Let them talk about you in such a way it brings a smile to their faces. Let your name and the memories of you evoke laughter and joy."

*Moment of Truth:*

*These quotes came to mind whenever I had conversations with my friends. They would always tell me just how much I made them laugh and brighten their day. My friends would call to tell me their troubles but end the conversation laughing, uncontrollably. Some told me that whenever they said or heard certain things on the television or radio they would think of me and smile.*

"Life...

It brings you sunshine and also rain, both have a purpose and both, if in abundance, can cause death and destruction. Do everything in moderation except when you do good to others. In fact, do lots of good for lots of people. You can never be too kind, too happy or too contented."

"Love Yourself, Be Content with what you have and Be Thankful for each day. Appreciate those in your life who stay because they Value You."

"Love cannot be contained...it cannot be killed off, it can be concealed but never destroyed...the more you stifle Love, the stronger it Grows. Love is defiant in the face of adversity...it is easily stirred, easily reignited. Love is everlasting."

"You pass by only once. Live your life to the Fullest, always doing everything possible to avoid hurting others and to make every effort to Love them knowing they are as imperfect as You are."

"Nothing is real but love. No matter how much wealth we acquire, no matter how famous we become, no matter how many continents we travel, the only thing that speaks to our heart, the only thing that can fill that space, is loving someone who values and who loves you right back."

"Love cannot be bought, stolen or borrowed. It is priceless and is True only when given sincerely and freely."

"Do not worry if they do not like you and show it, at least you know where you stand. Be worried if they say they love you and you still wait for them to prove it. You see, love is an action word and must be put into action. The love you speak about must be felt for it to be real."

"Like every living thing love requires certain things to keep it alive but not just to be alive, but to be vibrant, colourful and purposeful. Love is the ultimate dose of medicine for any illness. Keep it strong by treating it the way you want it to treat you."

"To love someone is not hard, in fact it is quite easy, just keep in mind that the focus is not what you can get but what you can give to make that person want to keep loving you...that way you both win at life and at love."

"It only takes a spark to start a fire,

It only needs rain to fall to end a season of drought,

It only takes a hug to show you care,

It only takes hate to start a war, and without a doubt, it only takes a smile to warm the heart and start a friendship."

"The right person for you will see the wall and break down walls to be with you, the wrong one will hide behind it."

# About Life...

"I want to experience the Peace that surpasses all understanding. I want to have Peace of Mind and to live in Peace with my fellowman."

PJW

"When others bring you war, speak with words of peace. When they show you hate, express love, for Love breeds love and Joy replenishes the heart. Feel your Joy increase."

*Moment of Truth:*

*There are going to be times when you feel like retaliating with the same weapon used against you. Those are the times you must not but instead, calmly and sincerely speak the opposite of what is being said to you. My ex placed my nude picture on the internet and I could have had him arrested and I was tempted to do so since he had me falsely arrested. It would have been sweet revenge but I chose not to, instead, I walked away knowing that his actions told more about him than it had of me. I felt a peaceful 'quiet' after I made the decision not to press charges. Let no one take your Peace.*

"To live in Peace with others, you first have to find the Peace within yourself. Inner Peace will not only give you a different perspective on any given situation, it will also allow you to exercise patience and tolerance towards those who may want to destroy that Peace which you have within you."

### Moment of Truth:

*I realised this when a family member was saying untruths about me and I was tempted to react, but I was not going to allow anyone to shatter the Peace I had found, which I so longed for. I told myself that because these words were not true and it required no self-evaluation or behavioural changes, then I ignored it and continued to show them that their untruths had no bearings or roots.*

"Those who let you down do not always mean to, do not be unforgiving, instead be understanding as misunderstandings are the causes of most conflicts."

### Thought Trail:

*You must always consider that people err and the people who love us will at times let us down. Be open to the fact that we too are fallible. Be willing to forgive and move on.*

"Peace, one of the very few things in life that money cannot buy. It is priceless that even the wealthiest among us cannot afford it. Cherish every moment of Peace you experience and give no one the power to take it away."

*Moment of Truth:*

*Living an unhappy and stifling marriage makes you value peace. It makes you content with the smallest of morsels and recognise what the real treasures in life really are. It was the many nights when I rode the buses that made me realise how priceless Peace really was and even though I was cold and uncomfortable I still preferred to be there than in a warm house with another spiteful human being.*

"You are too good and too worthy to allow your circumstances to defeat you."

*Think on This:*

*Circumstances change people, but it is people who are supposed to work at changing their circumstances. The same hot water that hardens egg softens potatoes.*

"Be conscious of your limits. There are people who cannot be helped, no matter what you do, how much you give of yourself, it will never be enough. For those people, the only and best thing you can do is wish them well and hope they find peace and open their hearts to receive and appreciate love."

*Moment of Truth:*

*After years of being kind and giving my best to a family member I realised that no matter what I did it was never enough and even when I went the extra mile, it was not even acknowledged. Rather than being hurt by it and making an issue of it, I just continued to do what was in my heart and accepted that no matter what I did, it would never be enough.*

"If the good you do will eventually come back to you, then clearly the bad will come back too. Think carefully on the medicine you dispense to others - bitter or sweet – because, maybe one day, you may just have to take it yourself."

*Think on This:*

*When we speak badly of people or treat them with disdain we open ourselves to being treated the same way by others. Be kind, the fruits of kindness are always sweet.*

Only when you accept failure as final, are you finally a failure. Anytime you learn from a failure you have taken a step towards Success. You cannot cross the finish line a winner unless you start the race and are ready to compete against your rival. Reach your full potential...tell yourself you are a Success.

*Think on This:*

*Your full potential can never be explored if you do not try.*

"Your best is always good enough. Strive to always do your best in everything you do. Do not let other peoples' success frighten you. Do not let it cause you to doubt yourself. You are only capable of being the best version of you."

*Think on This:*

*You cannot be someone else. You are only capable of being you and your best must never be compared to others. Your best is exactly what it is...your Best.*

"Only hard and tumultuous times determine how strong you really are. Your trials are necessary for your growth."

"The rough waters make for a better sailor, just as testing times bring forth a more powerful testimony."

"If it takes you to a place of hardship, it is preparing you to captain your own boat."

*Think on This:*

*If our journey is always smooth how can we be prepared for difficult times; yes, there are going to be difficult times and only challenges and trials can prepare you for them.*

"It is not the past that is important though it plays a part in shaping you; it is the now and what you do with it that determines a better future."

"Do not take your life for granted, those who left us yesterday had plans for tomorrow. Your today is that tomorrow. Appreciate each new day with renewed hope."

"Put your fears to rest, stop thinking of what can go wrong and allow your desires to be fulfilled by focusing on everything that can go right."

*Think on This:*

*Though our past is important in preparing us for the greater things to come; in order for us to succeed, we must cease the NOW moments and use the present opportunity to elevate ourselves to heights unknown.*

"When they throw bricks at you use them to build a wall that serves to protect you and improve your skills. Any obstacles or barriers in your way becomes a tool for you to use to manoeuvre your way to success."

*Moment of Truth:*

*This quote was born out of my many encounters with so many obstacles. It was these obstacles that drove me to do my research and it was these obstacles that caused me to detour and in so doing I met people who helped me and who encouraged me to fight and not give up. It was these barriers that pushed me to stand on my own two feet and led me to a place where self-belief was necessary for me to succeed.*

"When people come into your life and suddenly leave, it is simply because their part in your journey has ended, though your journey has not. People are placed at different paths to teach you lessons you need to learn, to strengthen you where you were weak and to encourage you. Learn from those who have left and embrace and appreciate those who are now here, their part may soon end too."

*Moment of Truth:*

*While going through my trials and being unjustly persecuted I met many people at different points during the five years. Each one of them having played their role. Once someone conned me out of hundreds of pounds but from that loss I learnt a few vital rules which helped me in court. Some of my friends abandoned me while others supported me. Not all of those people were still in my life but each played their role in my journey, teaching me invaluable lessons that have made me the person I am today.*

"Let your smile change the world of those around you, do not let the world around you dampen your smile."

*Think on This:*
*You have the power, do not allow other people's behavior to dampen your spirit, instead let your positive attitude have an impact upon their day.*

"Speak love instead of hate, speak joy instead of sadness. Choose peace instead of war. What you speak, you release."

"Speak positive words into your Life. Do not let negative words of others affect your mindset. Let your knowledge of SELF bring forth Success and Peace of Mind. Today, tell yourself nothing and no one has the power to change your Positive attitude.

Let your good vibrations be felt so much that it affects their attitude."

"No matter how positive you are about life there will always be people who will come into your space and try to kill your vibes, do not let them. Do not hand over your power to them. Let their negative chatter be drowned out by your Positive Vibrations."

*Think on This:*

*Do not let someone kill your vibes, you be the change factor, let your vibrations change their attitude and create a positive space for those around you.*

"In order to know your true strength you have to put it to the test. You have to go through the tough times, be driven by unbelievable challenges and know how much you can bear; you have to carry the weight...just like a weight lifter tries and lifts a little more at each attempt, so he knows how much he is capable of heaving. So too, you must push a little harder and walk a little further until you have reached your limit."

*Think on This:*

*Have you ever watched a weight lifting competition and see how the competitors add a little more weight to their bar on each lift? They will lift above their shoulders until they cannot lift the weight bar from the ground. At that point, they know they have reached their limit, for if they pushed too hard, it will only lead to an injury. Some will go away and for the next few months will train and try to lift the weight that defeated them for the next time.*

"The more you invest, the harder it is to let go but holding on can cause so much more loss and pain."

*Think on This:*

*Know when to let go of situations that take more out of you and drain you of your joy and peace.*

"A negative attitude towards any situation will always make it seem harder. Change your attitude before you try to change your circumstances. If your attitude remains the same you will view every situation difficult, if your attitude changes, your circumstances will seem less challenging and more manageable."

*Think on This:*

*When we approach an issue with negative thoughts we find that it is all doom and gloom. Finding workable solutions are more practicable if we approach it with a different mindset.... a positive one that is.*

"Rejection is not all bad...in fact it often leads to better people and wider roads. It offers you a newer perspective and should lead to self-evaluation. Rejection is not a sign that you are not good enough, as a matter of fact, often times it is because you are too good. Look at it with a different perspective and with far reaching lens. Yes, rejection many times takes you to a place of Acceptance and Promotion."

"When someone rejects you, it is not necessarily because your actions or your attitude are dubious, often times it is about them and their inability to handle or control you, also their unwillingness to accept your growth and your standards. Rejection is not always about you, sometimes it is about them and their inadequacies."

### Moment of Truth:

*I realise this when I had to walk away from my marriage. Even though I did the walking, I felt rejected. I felt rejected and that was why I walked. My ex did not reject me because I was a bad wife or lover, he rejected me because he could not control me or change me into who he thought I should be. His desire to change me was not because I was inadequate but because he felt inadequate. He felt I was too good for him. He questioned why I chose him when I could have had taller, stronger, richer and smarter. This led to many insecurities that greatly impacted upon how he treated me.*

Learn to PUSH through the pain and then PUSH past it, then slowly and steadily with conviction and self-belief PUSH towards your Purpose.

### Think on This:

*Pain is seen as a discomfort, an unwanted nuisance that cause you to hurt and to lose time, it takes away valuable time that you can use to be productive; it is an unpleasant and unwelcomed suffering. Yet, it is pain that teaches us the value of Laughter and Joy, teaches us about comfort and contentment. The pain we feel when we have been injured emotionally or physically is the same pain that makes us more resilient to further pain that teaches us about ourselves and what we are capable of withstanding.*

*It trains us in the same way a body builder prepares for a competition. No Pain...No Gain. The pain you endured, will later be revealed as a necessary lesson for us to be tougher, stronger and definitely more resilient.*

"A woman who can overcome the obstacles meant to ruin her is a woman on a mission with a passion that is steadfast and undeniable. She will not stop until she has won her battles or achieved her goals. Be careful not to underestimate such a woman, the more obstacles you put in her way is the stronger you make her. Removing those obstacles will be for her a challenge she is prepared to take on."

*Moment of Truth:*

*During the first three years of my separation I was faced with overwhelming obstacles as I tried to win custody of my children and keep my freedom. At first, it was very traumatic and it wore me down as each time I cleared one hurdle two more appeared in front of me. At this point I realised I had a choice, give up and lose my freedom and my children or keep clearing those barriers no matter how tiresome. Though I could not see the finish line I imagined myself crossing it.*

"Real life is about making mistakes and learning from them and therefore we cannot change the actions of our past, the times we wish we could erase. All we are capable of doing is trying our best to make sure that the next moment does not pass us by; so what we must do is ensure we take the first step towards the way things are and make them the way we desire them to be."

*Think on This:*
*You cannot change the past but you surely can take steps towards making sure you do not repeat the mistakes in the future.*

"If you are finding it extremely difficult to take the first step towards making your life the way you want it to be just focus on how to get there and not worry about when you will get there. Remember it is how you run the race that will determine if you win the race."

"Always keep in mind that it is not that you get there but how you get there. If you win the race by cheating, then you are not a true champion and can never boast of having integrity or diligence. Win with confidence and with truth, knowing you are a True WINNER in every way."

Use your time wisely, spend as much of it as possible doing the things you love. Be around people who value your company and not what you can do for them. Spend time with the people you can laugh with, those you can disagree with and still be friends.

*Think on This:*
*Your thoughts and actions are usually a reflection of what you practice. Therefore, spend it around people who have a positive influence on your life.*

"Let NOT the misery of other's effect your Joyous Spirit...instead let your Joy evoke laughter in their Souls and Love in their Hearts."

"Be Thankful for each Day and each Lesson. They have shaped you into who you are Today and if you are loving yourself more today than you did yesterday, then You are walking in the right direction."

Do it because YOU tell yourself YOU are Wonderfully made and God has a Purpose for You.

Do it because YOU know that no matter how hard life gets that YOU are able to overcome any obstacle with determination.

Your Purpose....

We have to live our lives to fulfil our purpose. If we try to live for others we will never reach our Destination. Help others along the way but never let their dream become your dream. Make your passion your Purpose. Find Your Purpose and reach Your Destination.

*Moment of Truth:*

*As I began to help my friend in his business, I allowed him to convince me that his dreams were mine, his plans were mine. I loved him dearly and wanted to help him but I was helping him to achieve his dreams and in doing so I forgot mine. I lost my focus for a while and wasted precious time putting aside my dreams to help him achieve his. We must always strive to help others but never forget our own dreams in the process.*

"In this life we mess up so often that sometimes we wonder if we are ever going to get it right. Welcome to Life and know that the only time you will get it right is when you start with what is on the inside. Address the issues which cause you to doubt yourself. The first step to change is 'Acceptance' and 'Self Belief'."

"It will happen. It may not happen in the time frame you want it to but just keep working at it.

Never Give Up on a Dream because you have convinced yourself you are too tired.

Refresh your mind with positive words of reinforcement and allow the power of those words to bring forth renewal."

Do not tear others down even when they have negative things to say about you. Sometimes people judge you by their own standards and treat you the way they feel about themselves. Spend time with those who whisper words of encouragement to you and drown out the negative talk of others.

It does not matter what they 'Think' it is all about your mindset. Are you bringing Joy instead of grief, Love instead of Hate, peace instead of War? Then, YOU are on the Right Track. Do not let their opinions determine who you are and what you stand for.

The road is often times rough.

The river crooked.

The tears keep coming.

The future seems bleak.

The hope lost.

The pain is all too intense.

When these are common features in your Life,

Focus on the lessons of the trials and you will learn to appreciate the calm after the chaos.

There are thieves of possessions and then there are those who steal joy. These people are a vexation to the spirit. Laugh regardless of the circumstances. Stay clear of people who wallow in their own misery and rejoice at your demise.

There is much that is not going right in your life. it may be pain, hurt, debts, emotional and physical issues or spiritual confusion...know that your life can still be filled with JOY and PEACE. Use the talents you were given and be reassured that you are equipped to deal with the challenges. Never lose sight of the fact that 'everything has its season' and your season will change. Take from today, the lessons though painful will empower you for tomorrow.

NO, I do not hate you...I cannot afford to; for doing so would mean I hate myself. For, you see, HATE consumes you, makes you ILL, makes you BITTER, makes you UNHAPPY and I Love myself too much to allow you to do that to me. Be aware that I Love You and while I may not like many things about you, it is too costly for me to HATE You.

Most people do not change because they think they need to but because they try to please others. That is why the change never lasts. Real change only takes place when the need to change is recognised and the desire to change comes from within.

*Think on This:*

*Have you ever noticed that people in your life who change their behaviour for a while but revert to their old mode of thinking, acting and speaking; that is because their need to change did not come from them recognising that their attitude affected their relationship with others.*

Remember that you are a unique creation; there is no other like you.

Remember to count your blessings, not your troubles.

Remember that nothing wastes more energy than worry.

Remember the longer you carry a grudge the heavier it gets.

Remember that people are treasures, not things.

Remember to take one day at a time.

Remember to show Gratitude

Remember a loyal friend is worth more than gold

Remember to love self and in so doing you can love others.

If you are in a position to help someone then Life cannot be all that bad. Someone will always be in a position to help you and you in turn can help someone else. Every person at one point in their life needs the support of another. No man is an island or can stand alone.

"Life is never as bad as we think it is. There is always a way...we just do not always see it and because of our failure to see it we are unable to find solutions to the problems which hinders our progress."

"Stuck? You can only move forward if you can recognise why you are stuck and what has caused you to remain in that position for so long, that it cripples your thoughts and kills your ambition. Take steps to move forward even if it is only the smallest of motions. Motion is Progress."

"Recognise your bad habits and flaws that impede your relationship with those close to you. To deny your shortcomings is to be your own worst enemy. Do not be complicit in your approach to your problem. You can only fix what is broken if you can see that it's broken."

*Think on This:*
*When we receive constructive criticism we must be mindful not to see it as an attack but as an observation. If you want to have better relationships with others you must take into consideration how you make them feel and if a flaw is pointed out, then make an effort to correct it, not defend it.*

"For the Trials I have been through...I am Wiser. For the battles I have fought, I am Stronger. For the challenges I have overcome...I am Bolder. SHOUT it from the mountain top...I am Wiser, Stronger and I am Fighter. Speak Life into your Living."

"You are Awesome, Beautiful, Unique, a Queen, a Flower, a Goddess, a Precious Gem (whichever one you want to be) You are not to be taken for granted. You deserve Affection, Attention, Appreciation and Adoration. YOU are created to Give Love and to be loved.

You are WOMAN...You are Strong!

Let no one make you feel any less.

CELEBRATE YOU!"

*Think on This:*

*Every person placed along your path is important. Welcome them on their entrance, bid them farewell on their exit. Embrace the experience.*

"It is NEVER too late for anything unless you are Dead as only death brings finality, then it will not matter. BELIEVE in Yourself and Your ability to Get Through anything. While you have life you have hopes of achieving your Goals. Greatness is in your Destiny."

Sometimes it takes every ounce of strength you have just to get through the night and every bit of Courage just to face the New Day. Do not give up, do not give in. Never doubt your resolve and your God. Timing is everything. Patience is everything plus a bit more.

Do not let them steal your JOY.

Do not let them take your PEACE.

Do not let them change your Attitude to LIFE.

Do not let them Mess with your HEAD.

Do not Let them in if all they do is bring Negative VIBES.

Hold on to Your Sanity and Cherish your INTEGRITY

"You do not need what anyone else has. You have what God gave you and once you recognise your gifts and talents, use them wisely and you will see how GREAT your gifts are. Nobody's talent is GREATER than the other...You just NEED to USE it do GREAT things."

"Questions are the channels by which we travel to get to the truth. To get to the truth, the questions must be authentic and penetrating, anything else will only lead back to lies, lies do not foster growth and lack of growth will never bring you Success."

"The wall of doubts can be knocked down with one little show of faith. Faith can only strive when it is nurtured. Feed into your mind positive thoughts and watch that wall come crashing down."

"We all experience challenges, they make us who we are today and they are many times unwelcome. During these times you only need a little courage to push you to face your fears and deal with them. Courage is that dose of stimulus you need to overcome your fears and be victorious."

"People will hate you even when you have done nothing wrong to them. Do not be dismayed, it is a reflection of how they feel about themselves and the shortcomings in their lives. It is easier for them to hate you because they see you as stronger and wiser. They see the way other people react towards you and this makes them look and feel weak around you, it forces them to look at themselves and they do not like what they see. You then become what they wish they were and around you they feel inadequate and therefore their hate towards you is nothing but the feeling of failure within themselves."

*Moment of Truth:*

*At some point in your life you may question why someone does not like you when you have not wronged them. I discovered that there are people who because of their lack of confidence or self-belief will actually hate you to the point of trying to hurt you. This I experienced with a co-worker who did their best to tarnish my reputation simply because I wanted they wanted to be like me. After months of having to deal with the snide remarks, they were told in a public forum by another co-worker that they only disliked me because of my personality which they wished they could have. This came as a shock to them but after that they changed the way they treated me. A few months later they left the company, giving everyone a little token, except me. I have not seen them since.*

"It is your life. It is your story. Do not let anyone write it for you; don't let them fill your pages with their misconception of who you are. Take control and make each paragraph a step, each chapter a success and the book, a powerful testimony. Be the Author of your story."

"If you do not learn to do anything else in this life, learn to do this;

You can truly know the power of Peace;

Only when you have been to war with others and yourself."

## Peaches Joy Williams

# About Relationships...

"We must first seek to understnd what we are about before we can truly relate to someone else. For to be someones companion and intimate friend and to really relate to them; we must take time to discover what makes them tick. Seek to always value and appreciate those you have given that special place in your heart."

PJW

"If you are the only one in your relationship fighting to keep it alive, fighting to understand why it is not working as it should, then you are in the wrong fight."

*Think on This:*

*A relationship is about two or more people committed to giving it their best shot. You cannot make a person love you if they do not and you cannot make them want to try if they do not think you are worth it.*

"Set your own relationship goals. Do not ever envy anyone's relationship. People will show you a happy face while sadness reigns in their hearts. You never know what takes place behind closed doors."

*Think of This:*

*How many times have we seen celebrity couples displaying the perfect marriage and even some of our very close friends and family do so and within a blink of an eye after many years of marriage, they call it quits? And then hear them say how their marriage had been on the decline for several years. We should strive to set our own goals and make every effort to attain them.*

"From the very moment you choose to love someone and make it known to them, you become responsible for the condition of their heart. If you awaken the love in someone then you must stand by your word since it is now your duty to encourage, appreciate, understand and protect their heart from any selfish action you may be prone to display. Take care of the one you choose to love and do your best to maintain that love."

"The test of time can be seen in relationships that have weathered the storms, where fragile egos have been bruised but repaired, hearts broken but healed and many good times celebrated. Do not take your friend or partner for granted believing there will not come a time when they will turn and walk. Cherish them the way you want to be cherished."

"Loving someone requires a deep sense of commitment and responsibility. You have to be prepared to give more than you get. Love that is sincere and true gives without expecting. In a relationship if both parties are giving their all then no one is left feeling used or unloved."

"It is quite simple; these three things are Key to keeping the one you love happy. Give them the Triple A Treatment:

Let them feel Appreciated

Give them Attention

Show your Affection."

"Great relationships entail commitment, understanding and hard work. Its longevity is dependent upon the willingness of each person to make sacrifices and often times compromises. To get from it what you need, you need to put in what is required for it to last."

"Relationships will not last unless you are willing to nurture it. Do not expect an easy road filled with roses, remember roses have thorns but nonetheless their beauty is unequalled. Like a rose, it is delicate and needs attention, in order for it to grow and produce even more beautiful blooms."

"Walk with those you feel a genuine connection, if you later feel a disconnect because of their behaviour and lack of integrity; feel no obligation to stay."

*Think on This:*
*Sometimes in the early part of a relationship you feel connected because you have not yet learnt much about each other. As time goes by you get to know each other better and realise there are far more issues which you do not connect with. If you feel that you are not compatible, then do not feel guilty about walking away from it.*

"One of the hardest things to do emotionally is to let go of someone you love. One of the hardest lessons to learn is that someone you think you cannot live without can easily Live without you…and then you realise that someone you always think about rarely ever thinks of you…and you know…life goes on."

"The basics of a relationship begins with self. Love you first, then love others after…"

"Relationships are not perfect and never will be as long as they are entered into with imperfect people. So, do not expect perfection when you are not perfect. Work on it."

"A relationship is never guaranteed to work, but it's guaranteed to fail if you don't put in the work."

"A person who truly loves you will always do their best to see the good in you and be prepared to stick with you to make it work."

"If you are questioning why you are still with them, just look back to the beginning of the relationship and see what made you start in the first place; there lies the answer to your question."

*Think on This:*

*Did you enter into this relationship for the right reasons? What made you start and what would make you stop?*

"The quality of our relationships is dependent upon how much time and affection we are willing to invest in it."

*Think on This:*

*If you do not spend time getting to know each other you will never understand each other. A relationship cannot survive without understanding and it won't grow without affection.*

"No true relationship can survive if it is not nurtured, no matter how much you love someone if they do not love you back it will eventually die."

"A relationship can only be strengthened if both parties are committed to its growth and longevity and if both are ready to forgive the other's mistakes and move on."

## About Self-Belief...

"The first step you need to take in reaching your goals is to believe you can do it, along the way you may need motivation, support and encouragement but ultimately you must have self-belief"

PJW

"You are too good, too worthy to allow your circumstances to defeat you."

*Think on This:*

*Too often we consider ourselves not to be worthy of having or being the best because all our lives we have been told we were not good enough. Our circumstances may be extremely difficult but when we begin to see ourselves as worthy, we will triumph over them.*

"You are more than you think you are, you are capable of all the things your mind can imagine and more."

*Think on This:*

*Self-belief is a powerful antidote for doubts. What your mind can conceive, your heart can achieve.*

I do it because I have confidence in self and mostly because I know it can be done because others before have done it. I do it because I am 'Built for a Purpose'.

"Be all that you can be, remember the focus is not what others think of you but what you know about yourself. Live knowing that your closet friend is you and your biggest enemy is Fear. Tell yourself that your fears cannot get the better of you and Believe it."

"To truly get to the heart of the matter then it must matter to you but first you must be honest with yourself. Seek the truth from within. Accept nothing less."

"Be thankful for every experience whether good or bad because those experiences are essential to your growth as an individual. The importance of these experiences is evident when you can see how they become the springboard to your Success."

VICTORY can only be attained with the will to fight to the end, no matter what weapons are used against you, the enemy can only defeat you if you believe you have lost the battle before it's finished. Half the battle is won with weapons, the other half is won with might, insight and the Courage to go on.

"Believe that you are Great, not just great because you say so but great because you have it in you to do great things for people who do not feel so great about themselves."

"If you can still smile during the pain, the difficult times, the trials and the persecution then you have already won. Your Victory is your smile that pushed through the pain."

"If they say it cannot be done and you do it, then soon enough they will talk good about you or bad behind you. Either way they are talking about you because you DID it."

"The mountain is not just there to look at, its purpose is far greater. It is to provide you with the challenge of climbing to the top in order to prove your greatness."

*Think on This:*

*Use whatever is in your way to make you fiercer. Do not see everything as an obstacle, see them as a challenge.*

"Lift your voice and let them hear the words you have to say.

Know that you are powerful beyond your imagination.

Know your worth...Believe in you."

"Ready, Steady, Soar to a new height that cannot be ignored. Let no man or circumstances keep you grounded when you have wings to FLY."

*Think on This:*

*Do not allow what people say about you to limit you. Go to the heights you were destined to reach.*

"You will have days when you question your purpose and wonder if anything at all will improve, if the struggles will end and if your dreams will ever be realised and then you appreciate that you have life, hope, friends but most of all you have purpose and until that purpose has been served, You have got to keep going and never Give Up."

"You are more than good enough. You are anything you believe you can be. Believe that you are the BEST."

*Think on This:*

*Self-Belief must be present in order for you to achieve your goals.*

"It is well! These are not just three words, they are powerful words and together it is a declaration over your life. It is well simply means that you let go of everything that says otherwise and speak LIFE into your existence."

"Sometimes, we feel like we cannot go on because the pain is too much and the journey too long. Hold on...you are STRONGER than you think."

### Think on This:

*Try to remember the last trial you had. Did you think you could get through it? You did and you are here to prove it. Just see the obstacles as the dumbbells you need to strengthen your arms.*

"The situations we find ourselves in sometimes drive us to make hard choices. It is not looking good and there seems to be no way out and we are backed into a corner; that is when self-belief is imperative and we have to pull out every last resolve to make that decision...yes, that defining moment."

It is all in your mind...everything you need you have been given to fulfil your purpose. It is hard to recognise it when all your life you have been led to believe that you are not worthy. You have to prepare your mind to Believe it and then Work to Achieve IT!!

*Think on This:*

*There are people without feet who climb mountains. If you have a conscious mind, then, anything is possible if you just believe.*

"True contentment is feeling that you are amazing without needing anyone else's approval to feel that way. Only then can you say you truly know what happiness means."

## About Being Yourself...

"You must never change who you are for someone else, remember the person you are now and the person you will be in a few years will be a reflection of who you truly are...not who you pretend to be. Never try to imitate anyone. Be you...it is you who must live with yourself, everyone else has a choice"

PJW

"Better they hate you for who you are than love you for whom you pretend to be. You should not have to change yourself for others to like you. Those who truly love you will take you as you are and will embrace you for how you make them feel."

*Think of This:*

*At all times be real about who you are. Do not allow someone else's perception of you change who you are. In this life you will always have critics. Concentrate on those who love and appreciate you.*

"Some people do not know the value of your friendship until they have lost it. If they do not appreciate your presence, then let them feel the effects of your absence. Let your love shine so bright that they are dazzled by it."

*Moment of Truth:*

*After being friends with someone for well over ten years they decided they no longer wanted to be my friend and stopped communicating with me. Two years later I received messages to me via friends to let me know that they missed me and how happy they would be to rekindle our friendship. Under normal circumstances I would have obliged but too much had been said during those two years.*

"Be kind even if you are shown unkindness.

Be bold in the face of adversity.

Be wise even when foolish thoughts cloud your mind.

Be courageous even if the battle seems unwinnable.

Be the best version of you...no one else knows how to be you, but You."

"Don't forget that YOU are the most important person in your life. Take care of You. Be good to others because you have the heart for it...let kindness be a very visible attribute that gives off a light for all to see. Remember being sincere with others is a reflection of who you are."

"Every time you try to be like someone else you are denying who you were created to be, you are killing your dreams and shrinking when you should be growing into the Awesome You!"

"Your identity is not built into someone's opinion of you. Take that risk, travel that road, have wild fun, love passionately but do not let anyone dictate to you how you should live. Too often we are afraid to live because we are concerned about what other people think of us."

"Whenever you allow someone to make you feel insignificant by telling you that you cannot do it, you give them power to make themselves bigger. Some people will try to belittle you because they are not capable of doing it."

"Never compare your achievements to others...they may have settled for something else because they were not brave enough to be themselves. Be the only person you were meant to be ... Be You!"

*Think on This:*

*We never truly know what other people are thinking or what their journey is all about. When we try to be like others we are at risk of living someone else's broken dreams. While you are trying to be like them they are busy trying to be like someone else. They may even want to be like you.*

"Do the things you want because you like doing it, not because everyone else is doing it. Dare to be you...laugh uncontrollably, dance like you are crazy and wear whatever makes you comfortable."

"Many people live in the shadow of someone else; they copy the attitudes and the behaviour of others they view as better because they feel that they are not good enough to be themselves. Society helps to foster that with all this celebrity worshipping. Don't be a second rate version of another...Be the Best version of You."

"Life is short...Do not waste it trying to be like someone else. They may not even like who they are."

*Think on This:*

*While you are loving someone else and hating who you are, they are hating who they are and wishing they were someone else. Confused? Yes, life is all so simpler when everyone just be themselves, while accepting and embracing their uniqueness.*

There are people who actually dislike you because you are Strong. There are those who will dislike you because you are talented and then there are those who will dislike you simply because You are YOU. Do not feel the need to want to change to accommodate them, instead be stronger, be more creative and most of all Be Yourself.

"You cannot extract peace from a place where there is only war. You cannot build bridges if you have no material to work with. You cannot make a horse drink if it does not want to and You cannot be someone else without losing yourself."

Speak from your heart always and those who truly know you will embrace you and appreciate your forthrightness.

"To be amazing is not about looking amazing, it is not about feeling amazing. It is about making others feel amazing by just being in your presence. It is spreading that amazing feeling and keeping it going."

You do not need anyone's approval. You were approved by the one who created you. Do not let anyone peel off your seal of approval because they do not know the value of theirs. Know your worth and let others see it.

"That day when you can truly be comfortable and contended with who you are, is the day it won't matter to you about what other people think about you."

# Peaches Joy Williams

A Daily Dose of Inspiration

# About Dreams and Goals...

"Never let anyone convince you that your goals are not achievable. You are not what they say you are... you are what you believe you can be...Go ahead, be the BEST"

PJW

"Hold on to your dreams, make the effort to do things which will ultimately bring you closer to it. One day they could become your reality which was once only a dream."

*Think on This:*

*Never dismiss your dreams especially, if, when you do so, you feel empty.*

"One step at a time takes you where you need to be. Taking small steps is better than none at all. Never QUIT because you are afraid, instead let the fear disappear because you never QUIT."

*Think on This:*

*If you want to go somewhere you have to move, it does not matter how as long as you move forward. Take your time if you must, but never give up.*

"Channel your thoughts, think carefully about your actions, visualise your dreams. It is only when you move from ideas to actions that you can truly achieve Success."

*Think on This:*
*To succeed you simply have to put your thoughts into action. Make it happen.*

Feel the FEAR and do it anyway.

Your Fears are real but they do NOT have to STOP you from reaching your Goals.

Make your Goals BIGGER than your fears and watch your fears shrink to nothingness.

"Do it because YOU know that no matter how hard life gets that YOU are able to overcome any obstacle with determination. Your determination to succeed is essential to your Success."

"If the wall is an obstacle to your goal, then learn to knock it down, climb over it, walk around it or pull it apart piece by piece. Do whatever it takes to achieve your goals...it is your Choice."

*Think on This:*
*Your problem is as great as you perceive it to be.
Look at it as a detour not a detriment.*

"The obstacle is not the problem. The problem is in your head telling you that you cannot do it. Once you learn to conquer that problem then the obstacles become your stepping stones."

"Never allow people to derail your dreams with their bitter words."

Focus on your desires and your ambitions, not their negativity.

Channel your thoughts and turn those in to Actions which will bring you SUCCESS."

"There are those who try to kill your dreams simply because they allow fear to keep them from attaining theirs. They feel unaccomplished around you and will say and do things to discourage you. Be mindful of them."

"Every dream you have ever had is possible with hard work, courage, determination and Faith."

"To keep your dreams alive, you need to believe in them, take steps towards achieving them, speak of them, and most importantly you have to be prepared to take risk in order to see them realised."

"All your dreams are possible as long as you have the determination to pursue them, the imagination to visualise them and the willingness and courage to take risk to achieve them."

"Once you keep believing in yourself and you maintain a positive attitude especially in the face of adversity, you are already on your way to making your dream come true."

"To complete a journey you first have to start it, to start it you have to take the first step, to take the first step you have to believe you are capable of doing it and that only takes an ounce of faith in your ability to achieve what your mind can perceive."

"Broken hearts can be mended, faded smiles can brighten, wounds can be healed and minds can be changed. Now go out there and revive those dreams of yours which you have buried."

Consider your journey through life as a bus ride to your destination. Know that some people will get off before you get there, some will stay for the entire ride; some may even make the ride more difficult, but when they disembark they will make space or those who will get on and stay with you to your destination.

# Peaches Joy Williams

"Close your eyes and dream of where you wish to be."

# About Life Lessons...

"Each experience and each person we meet have a lesson to teach us...learn it well"

PJW

"Stand Taller, Work Harder, Dream Bigger, Love More Passionately, Fight Fiercer, Walk Further and Stress Less about the trivial things in Life and then watch your Smile last longer."

*Think on This:*

*Each time you allow the little things to get you down, you become more stressed and miserable about your life.*

"Even the worst circumstances have a lesson or lessons to teach us. The solution is to be open to the idea of learning the lessons while handling the circumstances."

*Think on This:*

*Every obstacle and every challenge teaches us a lesson. Some are quite painful so we may not see it as a lesson until that time comes when we can look back and smile at our fear and pain.*

"Wear the right attitude, your success is dependent upon your attitude; your attitude is dependent upon your thoughts. Now that you know this...what thoughts will you allow to reside in your mind today?"

*Thought Trail:*

*Ever heard the saying your latitude is determined by your attitude? This is applicable in all walks of life, in your relationship, at work, at home and abroad.*

"Never regret anything, it is the mistakes and the bumps in the road that makes your journey and it is the people you have met and the experiences you've had that make you who you are today. Embrace your experiences and continue to use them to grow. Growth means that you have lived, lost and learnt, if you have learnt and you have lost then you are now Wiser and Stronger and that right there is valuable experience which can be used to your advantage."

*Think of This:*

*If it did not kill you, it has the power to make you stronger.*

"Any obstacles or barriers in your way become a tool for you to use to maneuver your way to success."

*Moment of Truth:*

*Each time we have to push down or push past a barrier we become more versatile, resourceful and adaptable. All these pave our way to success.*

"There comes a time when you will need to examine the way you allow others to treat you. If you are feeling inadequate around them then ask yourself why and take steps to change the situation."

*Think on This:*

*If you find that you allow others to mistreat you too often, then you must address the issue and if you must; walk away.*

"Embrace the lesser times, appreciate them, it is those significant but simple moments that we often cherish and hold dear to our hearts; like watching our children taking their first step, or seeing someone smile after recovering from an illness which made them sad and tearful. It is those little moments that give you the Greatest of Joy and brings great value to a smile."

*Think on This:*
*Appreciate and cherish the little things that money cannot buy, like a genuine smile or a warm and sincere hug. Life is simple; it is us who make it complicated.*

"The foolish man will never be blamed for his foolish actions, it is expected of him to be just that but the wise and prudent man will be chastised for his foolish mistakes. Remember where much is expected; much must be given."

Many times we are placed in situations where we lose control and find ourselves at the mercy of another. In times like these we have two choices, challenge them and face the consequences which may go in our favour or allow them to continue to intimidate and manipulate us, the latter choice has only one conclusion...your life is no longer your own and you have now lost the right to choose."

"Know when to call it quits. It is not always a negative thing, for sometimes when we are faced with a difficult task such as trying to please someone who is never satisfied then we place ourselves in a position to fail. It is always good to quit something that has a negative impact upon our minds and body. Quitting is always necessary and becomes the only solution if holding on will ultimately lead to self-destruction."

"Along Life's journey some very important people will appear, some to hurt you, some to help you, some to criticise you, some to comfort you, some to guide you and some to just Love you for who and what you are all about. Thank everyone who has played their part...without them your LIFE Story would be incomplete and uninteresting."

"Love life and be kind to others even to those who made it difficult for you to love them. Give of yourself but never give away the part that guides your conscience and never sell your soul for money, position or false pride. Your mistakes can never be erased but once you recognise and accept your shortcomings and are willing to move forward, then your restoration will be more powerful than any wrong doing."

"Learn to walk away from anything or anyone that steals your joy and burden your soul. Whoever or whatever you attach yourself to becomes a part of you as that which drains you cannot uplift you, that which take your peace can only bring you discontentment and anyone that does not celebrate with you cannot truly mean you well. Be wary of the company you keep; they can be a deterrent to you getting to your destination."

Today's the tomorrow you were looking forward to. Embrace it and do not lose sight of the goals you set yesterday. Act now! Procrastination will only delay you but cannot STOP the inevitable.

"It is never good enough to give a little and to expect that a lot will come back. While some may get away with being mediocre, know that it is never seen as extraordinary or outstanding. Hard work with commitment and the need to succeed is the only thing that will bring you true Success."

"We do not always get what we want but that does not mean we cannot give of ourselves fully. Do not give with the expectation to get. What we give out to others will always speak of us and about us long after we are gone."

"One of the hardest things to live with is the knowledge that you could do so much more with your life but were too afraid to take the chance and missed the opportunity that was right in front of you - that could have taken you exactly where you truly wanted to be."

"If we could turn back the hands of time some of us would be constantly on rewind and therefore would never move forward to our Destiny."

"We all deal with pain differently, to accept that other people's way is just as noteworthy and pertinent is proof that you have grown and learned from the experience."

"Toxic people can never see the good in any situation; they can never bring light to the dark, instead they will pull you into the dark with them. Avoid them!

"You will not be everyone's cup of tea and that is okay, remember, some people only like coffee."

The mouth does not always express what the heart feels, sometimes people hide their true feelings so as not to get hurt, so be careful not to take every word literally.

"When you are feeling infuriated or annoyed; that is never the best time to speak."

"If you feel it with your heart, then say it with your mouth and prove it by your actions but never with the intention to hurt or offend."

Be Bolder than you were before, Wiser and Stronger, Fiercer and Kinder. EVERY experience in this life, no matter how insignificant it may seem had something invaluable to teach you. Do NOT push them aside...Learn the lesson it was meant to teach.

Have you woken up feeling like you wished you can just sleep some more and sleep away your troubles? Are you wondering when will your situation ever going to improve? Are you feeling like you are stuck and frustrated? Be conscious of the fact that it is just a feeling and feelings can change. Do not let your emotions control how you live out your week...instead take control of your feelings and emotions, be the Master of your Destiny.

"I did not get my own way today,
But I have learnt that my way is not always the best way and now is not always the right time."

"Along your journey, you will find that there are those who cannot handle you because of who you are, they will walk away. Your honesty will always be welcomed by those who can handle the truth. Never watch your words for those who live a lie."

"You cannot put new food onto a dirty plate filled with stale food and expect it to be fresh. It is just the same way you cannot be a better version of you if you continue in your old way of thinking. Where new thoughts and ideas fail to be planted, old ways will continue to flourish."

"A thief of time is also a thief of life, for the quality of your life depends on the amount of time you spend doing what you love, in peace and with good intentions. Those who waste your time with negative chants waste your life."

"Sometimes the most powerful answer to a question is Silence."

"Release the contentions of yesterday, welcome the new challenges of today and look forward to the surprises tomorrow will bring."

"Time, the master of all things. The revealer of truths. It has a majestic way of revealing to us the important things which we too often overlook and reject; like the value of friends when we are lonely and alone surrounded by all the money we accumulated when we were too busy for friends."

"Do not force anything, not friends or any other relationships. Do not try to manipulate a situation or someone, if someone wants you in their life, they will let you in. If you enter someone's life through deception, then you will eventually leave in shame."

"I am my past. I am what I have been through. All these Struggles, Joys, Triumphs, Challenges and Rejection worked together to make me who I AM today."

"The only position some people want to see you is flat on your face. They take pleasure in your downfall and secretly wish you would stay there. Only a few genuinely care, the others just pretend to in order to know more about you, not to know you better. Choose your company wisely."

*Think of This:*

*Those who cannot smile at your victory have no wish to see you succeed.*

"Success is never about how much you have in the bank or who you know. It is about what you had to overcome to be where you are today. Not everyone wants to be a Doctor, Lawyer or Prime Minister. Some people are happy just being good people, loyal, loving, kind, giving and truly sincere without a fancy job title. It is better to be the best Janitor than be the worst Prime Minister. Your job title does not define you."

*Think on This:*

*What you do and who you are as a person are two different things. There are many people who are respected because of the job they do at their place of work, but are very unloving and uncaring towards their families at home. An abusive husband can sometimes hold the title of Doctor or Lawyer while a very caring father and loving husband holds the title of Street Cleaner. Do not respect people because of a title, respect them for who they are and how they treat you.*

# About Peace of Mind...

"There is nothing on this Earth that can make you contented, if you do not have peace of mind"

PJW

"If it eats away at your conscience and it hurts when you think about it, then it is time to address and confront the issues that rob you of your peace of mind. Nothing is liberating as a clear conscience."

*Think of This:*
*Whatever steals your joy can also imprison you.*

"Do not determine your worth by how other people treat you. Many people feel no self-worth and will find it difficult to treat you as the Prince or Princess that you are. Look inside and ask yourself these questions."

Am I being kind?

Am I being true to self and others?

Would I be happy with being treated the way I treat others?

If the answer to all is yes, then carry on doing what you have always done.

"Anything that steals your Joy and Peace of Mind needs to be re-evaluated and you MUST decide if it is worth keeping. Can you tolerate it and can you live without it? Most importantly you MUST realise that time spent on trying to fix the unfixable will not be given back to you. So, are you willing to be miserable just to hold on to people and things that steal your Joy? Let go and remember you don't get a second life."

*Think on This:*

*If it makes you miserable most of the time...Let it go.*

"Having Peace of Mind is the ultimate in having peace. Do not allow another to steal that from you because you are who matters, nobody else. Seek peace and it will find you.

*Think on This:*

*Whatever saps or drains you of your happiness cannot be good for you. Remove yourself from anything that steals your joy.*

A Daily Dose of Inspiration

## My Butterfly

In choosing an image for this book I had no doubt that I wanted to use a butterfly to portray my story, so that it gave my quotes true meaning and life.

A butterfly represents major changes and extraordinary growth, since the process and transformation it goes through, is arduous and difficult but necessary.

On being born, a butterfly is encased in a cocoon. It is in this confined, restricted space that its freedom of movement is limited and yet, this process is crucial for the caterpillar/pupa to be transformed into a beautiful creature, adorned with the most magnificent of colours. Not only is the butterfly beautiful, it usually has wide expansive wings which allow it to fly freely and enjoy the liberty it lacked while being bound. The struggle it takes to exit into this new dimension, it finally is not only beautiful to look at, but also one of Mother Nature's and the Earth's most delicate and purposeful of creatures.

Once it has pushed forth, it is ready for flight, recognising it has won its hardest battle yet.

## About The Author: Peaches Joy Williams

Peaches Joy is an entrepreneur. The owner and operator of her business 'Occasions-Events', she provides services in event planning, children's entertainment/party hosting, face painting, and floral designs (for weddings, corporate events and other social events). A woman with many talents, she uses these to enhance her services on a professional level and also in her personal life. Among Peaches' many other talents, she is a proud and keen gardener, interior decorator, caterer and now a captivating author.

Born and raised in Jamaica, she hails from the capital, Kingston. Immigrating to the UK in the 90s, she embarked on starting a family. Now divorced, she lives with her three adult children.

This is not Peaches Joy's first piece of literary work. She is a bestselling co-author and also an avid poet and she hopes that one day, she'll publish her collection of poems.

A trained teacher and certified florist, she holds a Diploma in Education, Diploma in Floristry and Bachelor of Arts in Community Development and Education. Peaches Joy boasts skills and experience in several fields with also assuming roles as a probation officer, women's refuge coordinator and family liaison worker. Fond of children and during her years as a teacher, Peaches has touched the lives of many children since her desire to help them is embedded in her passion to run her own charity for disaffected young people in her homeland of Jamaica. She is presently taking steps to set up her Charity 'Melody's Mission' in the island and in the memory of her sister who was a dedicated Social Worker. In addition, she is making plans to start a charity for the homeless in her local community, called 'Socks and Sandwiches'.

Peaches Joy boasts a strong spiritual belief in God and credits her resilience and courage to her faith. Peaches Joy believes her faith is what has carried her through the difficult and tumultuous times leading to her success. Peaches Joy is all about making a difference and hope to do so on a grander scale by getting her message across to as many young people as possible about their worth and value to society. She hopes to embark on making it her mission to encourage and train young people using the many skills she possesses.

Peaches Joy Williams can be contacted at:
peachesjoy.ptp@hotmail.com

www.ingramcontent.com/pod-product-compliance
Lightning Source LLC
Chambersburg PA
CBHW071722040426
42446CB00011B/2183